DINO SAFARI

GRAB YOUR GEAR AND JOIN THE ADVENTURE!

ARCTURUS

Picture credits:
Cover: pixel-shack.com.
Corbis: 46–47, 49br, 65, 70–71 (composite with pixel-shack.com), 74–75, 95. De Agostini
Picture Library: 13tr, 13cr, 15cr, 17br, 19br, 21tr, 25cr, 25br, 27tr, 29cr, 31br, 33tr, 33cr, 33br,
103tr, 103br, 109br, 111cr, 115tr, 115cr, 115br, 125. Dorling Kindersley: 66–67, 72–73,
8–83, 83tr, 83cr, 88–89, 92–93, 93cr, 95. Highlights for Children, Inc.: 13br, 21cr, 25tr, 111tr.
iStockphoto: 17tr, 17cr. Martin Sanders: 4–5, 8–9, 38–39, 68–69, 98–99. Miles Kelly Publishing
Ltd.: 19cr, 29tr, 29br, 107cr, 107br, 111br, 113br, 117tr. National Geographic: 120–121,
121tr, 121cr. Natural History Museum: 19tr, 21br, 27cr, 27br, 103cr, 109tr, 117cr. pixel-shack.
com: 6–7, 11tr, 12–13, 14–15, 18–19, 20–21, 29–29, 30–31, 31tr, 34t, 36–37, 41tr, 42–43,
43cr, 44–45, 48–49, 50–51, 52–53, 54–55, 56–57, 60–61, 62–63, 64t, 65, 70–71 (composite
with Corbis), 71tr, 76–77, 77tr, 84–85, 85tr, 86–87, 94t, 95, 96–97, 101br, 104–105,
106–107, 107tr, 108–109, 110–111, 112–113, 113cr, 114–115, 116–117, 118–119, 119tr,
122–123, 124t, 125. Science Photo Library: 51tr, 51br, 53br, 55tr, 58–59, 77cr, 77br, 78–79,
79tr, 79cr, 89tr, 90–91, 95. Shutterstock: 2–3, 10–11, 11cr, 11br, 16–17, 22–23, 23tr, 23br,
24–25, 26–27, 32–33, 35, 40–41, 41cr, 41br, 43tr, 47cr, 47br, 53tr, 61tr, 65, 71cr, 71br,
73tr, 73cr, 80–81, 81cr, 81br, 87tr, 95, 100–101, 101tr, 101cr, 102–103, 105cr, 105br, 113tr,
119br, 123t, 123cr, 123br, 125. Wikimedia: 15tr, 15br, 23cr, 31cr, 34b, 43br, 45tr, 45cr, 45br,
47tr, 49tr, 49cr, 53cr, 55br, 57tr, 57br, 59tr, 59br, 61br, 63tr, 63br, 65, 73br, 79br, 81tr, 83br,
85cr, 85br, 87cr, 87br, 89cr, 89br, 91tr, 91cr, 91br, 95, 109cr, 117br, 119cr, 121br.

ARCTURUS

This edition published in 2012 by Arcturus Publishing Limited
26/27 Bickels Yard, 151–153 Bermondsey Street,
London SE1 3HA

Written by Paul Harrison
Edited by Joe Harris
Picture Research by Joe Harris
Designed by Emma Randall

ISBN: 978-1-84858-542-3
CH002253EN
Supplier 05, Date 0912, Print Run 1615

Printed in Singapore

CONTENTS

WELCOME TO THE PAST...

Somewhere deep in the ocean lies a group of very special islands. Here, the dinosaurs from millions of years ago are alive and kicking. Scientists have only briefly scouted from the air. Now, your mission is to spend five days exploring these islands, recording your experiences and filming all the dinosaurs you find.

It will be dangerous. You will have a support team staying on a ship but they will be too far away to help. Once on the island, you will be on your own.

Are you ready to meet the dinosaurs?

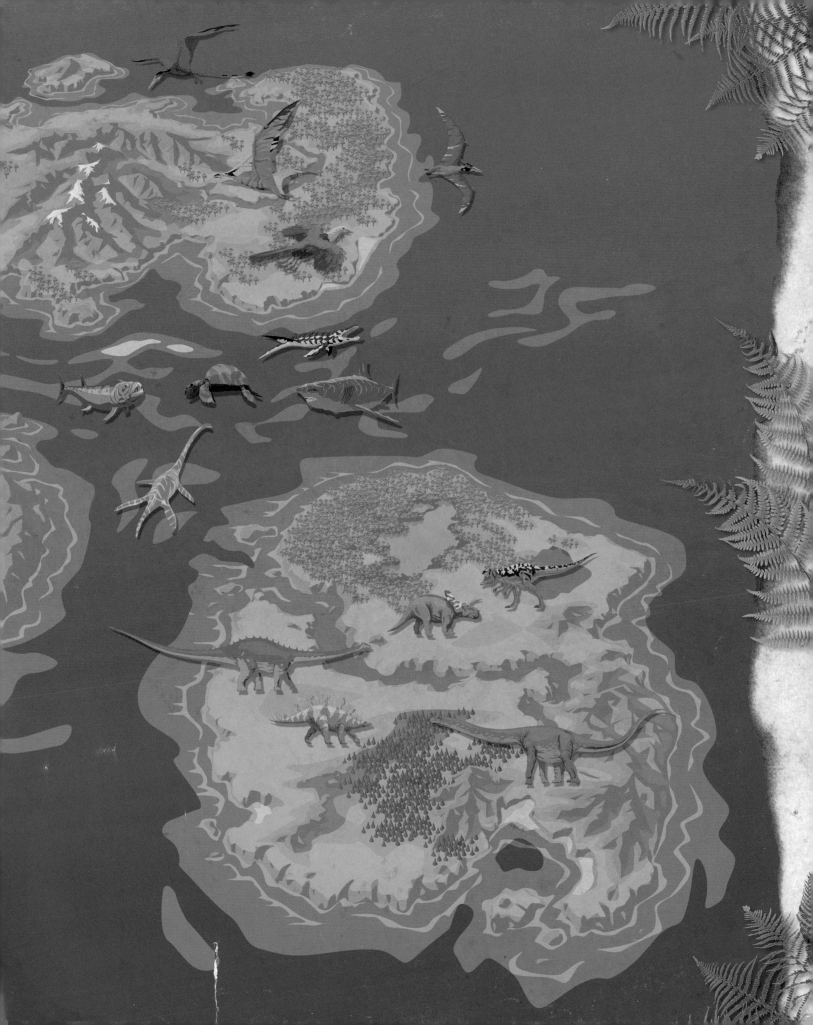

GIANT DINOSAURS

Are you ready for a truly breathtaking adventure? You are about to arrive on a secret island – an island full of huge prehistoric monsters. Your goal today is to capture the biggest dinosaur of all on film. Your tracking skills, your sprinting ability and your bravery are going to be essential.

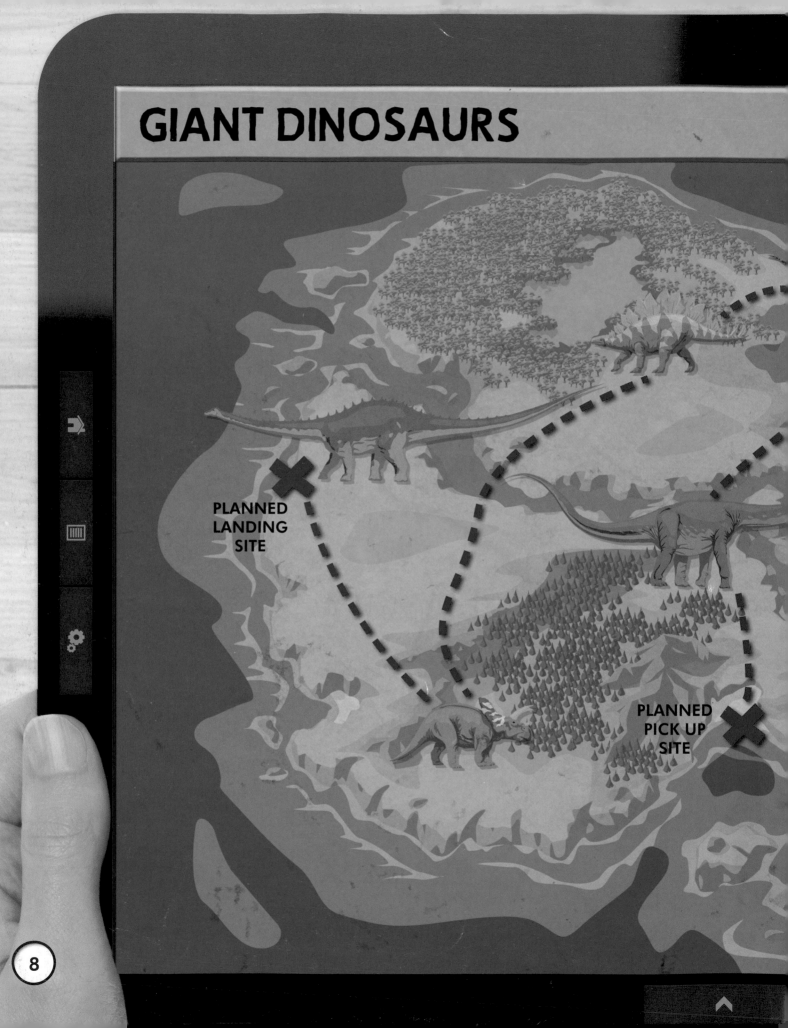

GIANT DINOSAURS

PLANNED
LANDING
SITE

PLANNED
PICK UP
SITE

You check your map one last time before you set out.

DINOSAURS TO SPOT

N
W ◆ E
S

▲ **Diplodocus** This huge beast needs lots of room. It may be found on grassy plains.

▶ **Triceratops**
Herbivore
Triceratops will be
near bushes and
other low vegetation.

◀ **Stegosaurus**
This dinosaur needs
warmth and good
grazing.

◀ **Gigantosaurus**
Look by the lake
for this carnivore,
as it likes to stalk
prey near the
water.

▲ **Argentinosaurus** This mountain-sized dinosaur may be near the actual mountains!

GIANT SAFARI

Your adventure begins with a parachute jump from a plane onto the island. The pilot circles low, looking for the right spot. You stare from the window, amazed that the island is home to creatures that are meant to have died out 65 million years ago.

As you fly over the island, a group of flying reptiles swoops dangerously close to your plane. They must be *Pteranodons*.

Soon you will be facing huge heavyweights like *Triceratops*. These creatures might be plant-eaters, but they could easily flatten you underfoot or impale you with their horns.

The size of the soaring *Pteranodons* takes your breath away. Their wingspan is bigger than any modern bird alive today.

SAFARI ESSENTIALS

Gingko leaves Some of the biggest dinosaurs are plant-eaters, so tasty leaves from this tree might prove a useful distraction. Gingkos are called 'living fossils', as similar plants existed up to 270 million years ago.

Camera Your friends are unlikely to believe what you see on safari – so you will need lots of photos as proof. A good zoom lens means you won't have to get too close.

dinoPad All the dinosaur facts you need to know have been downloaded onto your electronic reader.

LONG NECKS

The parachute drop is over in seconds. The breeze carries you down onto a wet, sandy beach, right next to a herd of gigantic *Brachiosaurus*. They call to each other – do they see you as a threat? You back away from their powerful tails and quickly gather up the parachute. Then you follow the giants as they amble along the beach, into a forested area.

Brachiosaurus is much higher than a house, and it can stretch its long neck to graze on the topmost leaves of conifer trees. It leaves footprints 3 ft (1 m) long.

Its chisel-like teeth are good for cutting but not chewing. To help digest tough leaves, it swallows stones that grind the greens in its giant-sized stomach.

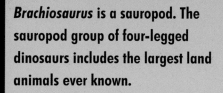

Brachiosaurus is a sauropod. The sauropod group of four-legged dinosaurs includes the largest land animals ever known.

Meaning of name: Arm lizard
Height: 53 ft (16 m)
Length: 99 ft (30 m)
Family: Brachiosauridae
Period: Late Jurassic
Weight: 88 tons (80,000 kg)
Found in: Algeria, Portugal, Tanzania, USA
Diet: Plants

GRAZERS

Many of the biggest dinosaurs are herbivores (plant-eaters).

▼ *Alamosaurus*
In spite of its size, the powerful back legs of the *Alamosaurus* are strong enough to take its full weight when stretching to reach the topmost branches of trees.

▶ *Iguanodon*
The plant-eating *Iguanodon* has tough teeth in its beak-like mouth for grinding up plants.

◀ Prehistoric plants
Flowering plants did not become common until the Cretaceous period. Before that, sauropods had to feed on tough-leaved evergreens, such as conifers and cycads.

SPINY HUNTER

You slip cautiously through the sharp-leaved plants to a sunlit swamp, where you come across a huge predator. The creature – a *Spinosaurus* – is peering into a pool of water. Suddenly it snatches up a fish. You see sharp teeth and catch the stench of its foul breath. Then it turns and looks straight at you. Time to make a quick escape!

Unlike other meat-eating dinosaurs, spinosaurids have a long, narrow snout and small, sharp teeth — useful for snapping up slippery fish.

Spinosaurus eats mainly carrion and fish. The big claws on its thumbs are used for fighting and to grasp fish.

The 'sail' of skin and bone on the *Spinosaurus'* back might be used like a solar panel to help heat up its body and a car radiator to cool it down, or for display.

SAILS AND FINS

▶ **Spinosaurus**
The sail of *Spinosaurus* contains spines that stand up from the backbone up to 6.5 ft (2 m) high.

▼ **Acrocanthosaurus** is a killer with a small fin down its back. This is thicker than *Spinosaurus*'s sail and might be used for fat storage or signalling.

▼ **Dimetrodon** The 10 ft- (3 m-) high *Dimetrodon* is the most aggressive predator of the Permian period. It has an impressive sail that must terrify its prey.

Spinosaurus, a theropod, is probably the longest (but not overall biggest) meat-eater to walk the planet.

Meaning of name: Thorn lizard
Height: 17 ft (5 m)
Length: 52 ft (16 m)
Family: Spinosauridae
Period: Late Cretaceous
Weight: 4 tons (3,600 kg)
Found in: Egypt, Morocco
Diet: Meat

MONSTER FOOTPRINTS

You run until you are out of breath, and clear of the trees. Soon you find a set of prints, which you start to follow. Before long, you discover the source of the trail – a herd of *Diplodocus*. You used to think of these as gentle giants, but now realize their tails are powerful weapons. Something flashes before your eyes! You crouch to avoid another crack of the 'whip'.

Diplodocus' pencil-sharp teeth, downturned head and long neck are used to feed on a wide area of low-growing plants. It grazes like a cow.

There are nostrils on the top of its head — useful to sniff the air for likely predators as it grazes.

The head is small compared to the body, with room for just a tiny brain. It is not very intelligent.

Diplodocus is one of the most famous dinosaurs and travels in grazing herds.

Meaning of name: Double beam
Height: 16 ft (5 m)
Length: 89 ft (27 m)
Family: Diplodocidea
Period: Late Jurassic
Weight: 12 tons (11,000 kg)
Found in: United States
Diet: Plants

FEET AND FOOTPRINTS
Fossil footprints show how dinosaurs walked.

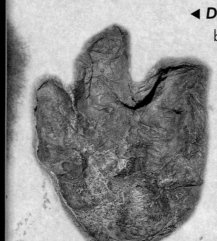

◄ *Diplodocus* leaves huge back footprints and smaller front footprints. It walks on thick pads and three toes, built to take the weight of its massive body. The front feet have sharp thumb claws. It walks slowly.

► *Tyrannosaurus* and other meat-eaters leave large, bird-like footprints. They move on two legs, and can run fast. Three of the four toes on each foot touch the ground.

▼ *Triceratops* leave smaller prints than long-necked sauropods, but their depth shows the heavy weight of their bodies. They are slow, plodding walkers.

GIANT EGGS

While crouching, you spot something that looks like a white football. As you look closer at the 'ball', you realize it's a huge egg. Then you see another, and another. The last is warm, recently laid. A few more steps and there's the spectacular egg-layer – an *Apatosaurus*, even sturdier looking than a *Diplodocus*. It wanders off, leaving the eggs to hatch alone.

Apatosaurus does not take care of its eggs or its newly hatched young. The eggs are an easy meal for predators.

Apatosaurus lays its eggs as it walks, each egg dropping about 8 ft (2.5 m) onto the ground without breaking.

Apatosaurus eggs are up to 1 ft (30 cm) in diameter.

Apatosaurus (once known as a *Brontosaurus*) is a massive sauropod, but harmless — unless it steps on you.

Meaning of name: Deceptive lizard
Height: 13 ft (4 m)
Length: 70 ft (21 m)
Family: Diplodocidea
Period: Late Jurassic
Weight: 33 tons (30,000 kg)
Found in: United States
Diet: Plants

EGGS AND NESTS

▶ Eggs are a perfect meal for a beaky dinosaur like *Gallimimus*. Its long, toothless jaws can easily crack the shell of a small dinosaur egg.

▼ Most dinosaurs lay their eggs in nests (a mound of soil or mud), like *Maiasaura* (which means 'good-mother lizard'). *Maiasaura* may look after their young for years and travel with them in herds.

▼ The biggest dinosaur egg fossils ever found are ellipsoid in shape and 16 in (40 cm) long.

WALKING TANKS

You soon come across four awesome, horned monsters – the tank-like *Triceratops*! These creatures seem to be on edge, so you are relieved to remember they are herbivores. You witness a head-to-head combat between two males. Horns crack and crash. The whole forest shakes as another joins in. It's time to beat a hasty retreat, before you are trampled...

The three sharp horns are used to battle with other males as they fight over mates. They are also useful for fighting off predators. By stabbing the underbellies of dinosaurs like *Tyrannosaurus* they can escape.

The frill protects the vulnerable neck from a deadly bite, tearing claw or jabbing horn.

Triceratops' teeth are like shears, perfect for chomping through low-growing plants.

Triceratops is a fearsome, three-horned plant-eater.

Meaning of name: Three-horned face
Height: 10 ft (3 m)
Length: 30 ft (9 m)
Family: Ceratopidae
Period: Late Cretaceous
Weight: 6 tons (5,400 kg)
Found in: United States
Diet: Plants

FRILLED FACES

▼ **Chasmosaurus** has a huge, rectangular neck frill. Instead of solid bone, which would have been too heavy, it is made up of bone struts, with skin stretched across.

◄ **Styracosaurus** can form a protective wall with their 2-ft- (60-cm-) long horns and frills, by gathering in herds. The younger, more vulnerable, Styracosaurus are protected by staying near the middle.

► **Centrosaurus** has a frill that is too thin to protect its neck. Instead, it may have been for show, to scare off predators or to attract mates. This skull shows the holes in the frill, which make it lighter.

DRAGON DINOSAUR

You follow a rustling in the trees – and almost run into the mouth of a dragon-like *Ceratosaurus*! You clamber up a conifer tree, but only just in time. You cling tight – one slip and you will be minced by those blade-like teeth. Suddenly the predator swings its head around, spots some easier prey and strides away.

The horns and jagged crest down the back of the *Ceratosaurus* are for show.

This giant can run fast to catch its prey, and has jaws large enough to kill at a single bite.

Ceratosaurus is one of the most common predators in late-Jurassic times, so where there is one, there are likely to be more.

Ceratosaurus is a member of the same family as **Allosaurus** and was at the top of the food chain where it lived.

Meaning of name: Horned lizard
Height: 13 ft (4 m)
Length: 20 ft (6 m)
Family: Ceratosauridae
Period: Late Jurassic
Weight: 1.4 tons (1,300 kg)
Found in: United States
Diet: Meat

The curved claws are well designed for giving deadly blows and for ripping the flesh from a carcass.

IN THE JAWS OF THE GIANTS

▶ Giant meat-eating theropods like *Tyrannosaurus rex* and *Ceratosaurus* have some of the biggest teeth – up to 9 in (23 cm) in length. They are pointed and sharp for tearing flesh and crushing bones.

▼ The largest hadrosaur, *Shantungosaurus*, has at least 378 teeth. Hadrosaurs have the most teeth of any dinosaurs, with rows of up to a thousand very small teeth lined up to chop through tough plants.

▶ Giant sauropods like *Apatosaurus* have small heads and teeth less than 1.6 in (4 cm) long. Their peg-like teeth are only useful for biting off leaves to eat.

PLATES AND SPIKES

Taking care not to be spotted, you observe the killer's new prey – a lone *Stegosaurus*. It thrashes its spiked tail and raises its plated back to warn off the predator. You are not surprised when the *Ceratosaurus* backs off, leaving the *Stegosaurus* to warm its kite-shaped plates in the afternoon sun. You sit down and eat your lunch.

The two rows of back plates are too weak to protect the dinosaur from an attack. They may help regulate the dinosaur's body temperature.

Its short neck means that *Stegosaurus* can only reach plants growing close to the ground.

Stegosaurus has the jaws and teeth to graze and grind. Its cheeks can store food for chewing later.

Stegosaurus **is the largest member of the plant-eating family of stegosaurs.**

Meaning of name: Roof lizard
Height: 9 ft (2.8 m)
Length: 30 ft (9 m)
Family: Stegosauridae
Period: Late Jurassic
Weight: 3 tons (2,700 kg)
Found in: United States
Diet: Plants

Stegosaurus can swing these fearsome spikes at an approaching predator.

BODY PROTECTION

▼ *Saltasaurus'* back is covered in small, horn-like bumps. There are strong, bony discs under the skin's surface.

▼ *Nodosaurus* is the height of an adult human. Like a tortoise, it can crouch under its bony plates and wait for any predator to tire of trying to break through.

▼ *Wuerhosaurus* has a spiked tail like the *Stegosaurus*, and two rows of back plates too. Stegosaur tails are called 'thagomizers'. Some bear up to ten deadly spikes.

CALL OF THE DINOSAURS

You are startled by a horn-like noise. Turning, you see a curious beast with a bright red crest – a *Parasaurolophus*. It blasts its 'horn' again, then a smaller creature comes thundering through the trees. It's a female, attracted to the sound of its mate. However, a huge predator has also heard the call of the duck-billed dinosaur. *Parasaurolophus* are its favourite prey...

Parasaurolophus is called a duck-billed dinosaur because its beak-like snout is similar to a modern duck's bill.

Meaning of name: Ridged lizard
Height: 9 ft (2.8 m)
Length: 33 ft (10 m)
Family: Hadrosauridae
Period: Late Cretaceous
Weight: 3 tons (2,700 kg)
Found in: Canada, United States
Diet: Plants

The swept-back, curved crest and tail form a streamlined shape that can slip between the undergrowth without being seen.

Tubes in the crest make the *Parasaurolophus'* call louder.

The larger crest means that other *Parasaurolophus* recognize it as a male.

A snort from this creature sounds like a blast from a horn or a trombone.

OTHER HADROSAURS

▼ **Corythosaurus** has a cutting beak and a mouth crammed with grinding teeth. Like other hadrosaurs it is a plant-eater.

▼ **Edmontosaurus** may inflate the loose skin around its nose to attract a mate, in the same way a toad blows up a pouch under its chin.

▼ **Lambeosaurus** is a herd dweller. Group living provides safety in numbers, and crests are a useful way of identifying family members.

DEADLY GIANT

Trapped between a *Giganotosaurus* and its prey, you stand frozen with fear. The hungry killer snarls from 36 feet (11 m) above. You nervously admire its clawed fingers, powerful jaw, vicious teeth and intelligent eyes. It moves slowly, staring at you and the hadrosaurs. It lurches forward, you scream... and then you are saved by a shadow.

Giganotosaurus are the largest known carnivorous dinosaurs.

Unlike *Tyrannosaurus rex*, whose teeth are shaped for crushing and tearing flesh and bone, *Giganotosaurus* has teeth that are flatter and more dagger-like, which work like meat-slicers.

Giganotosaurus is thought to be the largest theropod, but not the biggest dinosaur. Some plant-eaters tower over this dinosaur.

Meaning of name: Giant southern lizard
Height: 10 ft (3 m)
Length: 43 ft (13 m)
Family: Allosauridae
Period: Mid Cretaceous
Weight: 6 tons (5,400 kg)
Found in: Argentina
Diet: Meat

Muscular hind legs and a large tail for balance means *Giganotosaurus* can run fast, in spite of its weight.

BIG AND BRAINY?

A bigger brain in relation to the body of a dinosaur often suggests greater intelligence.

▼ *Tyrannosaurus rex* Although *T. rex* has a slightly smaller body than the *Giganotosaurus*, its brain is bigger. Both need large brains as hunting requires intelligence, good eyesight and speed.

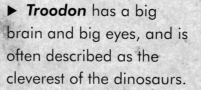

▶ *Troodon* has a big brain and big eyes, and is often described as the cleverest of the dinosaurs.

▼ *Stegosaurus* This huge creature's brain is the size of a lemon. Some scientists believe it may have another brain elsewhere in its body.

THE GIANT OF GIANTS?

The sky turns black as the dinosaur you've been seeking looms, casting a mountain-sized shadow. You blink, look up and see the magnificent form of what is probably the biggest dinosaur to have lived – *Argentinosaurus*. The *Giganotosaurus* almost drools at the sight of such a vast meal. Suddenly you are aware of being in the middle of what could be the most violent dinosaur battle ever, so you run for your life.

Colossal sauropods like *Argentinosaurus* need lots of food as they grow into adults. An adolescent probably gains as much as 100 pounds (45 kg) of weight each day.

Argentinosaurus, a sauropod, may be the tallest and heaviest land animal ever to have existed.

Meaning of name: Argentina lizard
Height: 70 ft (21.4 m)
Length: 120 ft (36.6 m)
Family: Antarctosauridae
Period: Late Cretaceous
Weight: 121 tons (110,000 kg)
Found in: Argentina
Diet: Plants

Argentinosaurus weighs more than 15 fully-grown elephants put together.

WEIGHING UP THE EVIDENCE

▶ *Argentinosaurus* Little has been found of this dinosaur, but scientists have estimated its size by measuring vertebrae (back bones). Many are 5 ft (1.5 m) tall by 5 ft (1.5 m) wide. That's as tall as an adult human!

▼ *Amphicoelias* will always be a contender for the biggest dinosaur, but the only fossil ever found has been lost – just a drawing exists (see below).

◀ *Seismosaurus* holds the record for being the longest dinosaur, at 130 ft (40 m), because of its impressive tail. However, *Argentinosaurus* was taller and heavier.

CAMOUFLAGE

The sun is setting. It's time to head for the shore, where a boat is due to pick you up and take you to the ship you are based on. You wade through the marshes and stop to gaze at familiar markings on unfamiliar creatures. Just as giraffes have camouflage, so do these giant sauropods! You know why they need to hide — you've met some of the terrifying predators they fear.

The *Dicraeosaurus* has an unusually short neck and relatively large head for a sauropod.

As on a giraffe, patches or spots help hide the dinosaur when it is amongst the shadows of trees.

Dicraeosaurus browse in areas with other plant eaters, *Giraffatitan* and *Kentrosaurus*. Because each of these is a different height, they eat plants at different levels, so there's no fighting over the juiciest leaves.

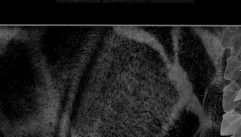

Dicraeosaurus is in the same family as *Diplodocus* and has a whip-like tail that it uses as a weapon.

Meaning of name: Two forked lizard
Height: 12 ft (3.7 m)
Length: 66 ft (20 m)
Family: Diplodocidae
Period: Late Jurassic
Weight: 6 tons (5,400 kg)
Found in: Tanzania
Diet: Plants

Like all dinosaurs, *Dicraeosaurus* could not swim, but probably waded into rivers for a drink, to cool down or to escape a passing predator.

PATTERNED DINOSAURS

What do we know about dinosaurs' skin?

▼ **Evidence** Mummified skin tissue from a 67 million-year-old hadrosaur shows that the dinosaur had skin scales of different sizes, suggesting stripes or other patterns. But until we know for sure, artists must use their imagination.

▼ **Camouflage** A heavy dinosaur like *Polacanthus* may have had markings that meant they could crouch and hide from predators amongst the undergrowth.

▶ **Feathers** Fossil evidence shows that many dinosaurs, such as this *Syntarsus*, had feathers for insulation or display.

GIANT SAFARI REPORT

On your way back, you look at the photographs you have taken on your first day. The picture that still makes you shudder is your snap of the *Giganotosaurus*. What could be more terrifying than a giant killer with teeth like sharp knives? And you were within inches of it!

Paleontologists are still trying to work out which of the giants is the size record-holder. New fossils and discoveries are being made all the time, which means a final decision is impossible. Some scientists believe that *Argentinosaurus* is the largest dinosaur ever to have lived. Others argue that *Amphicoelias* or *Bruhathkayosaurus* could have been even bigger (see below). In the future, fossils of even larger monsters may be discovered!

60 m

■ *Amphicoelias*　　■ *Supersaurus*
■ *Bruhathkayosaurus*　　■ *Argentinosaurus*
■ *Diplodocus*　　■ *Brachiosaurus*

The incredible inhabitants of your safari location originally lived at two different times during the prehistoric era.

JURASSIC 200 million to 150 million years ago

Stegosaurus

Dicraeosaurus

Apatosaurus

Brachiosaurus

Diplodocus

CRETACEOUS 150 million to 65 million years ago

Giganotosaurus

Ceratosaurus

Parasaurolophus

Spinosaurus

Triceratops

Argentinosaurus

FLYING MONSTERS

Today your mission is to find and film the flying reptiles that make another secret island their home. You will soar through the air, tracking these amazing creatures that are far bigger than any bird today. A good head for heights is essential on this death-defying adventure.

FLYING MONSTERS

PLANNED
LANDING
SITE

You check your map one last time before you set out.

N
W ◆ E
S

✖

**PLANNED
PICK UP
SITE**

DINOSAURS TO SPOT

◄ *Pteranodon* This winged reptile flies out to sea in search of fish.

◄ *Eudimorphodon* Although clumsy on land, it can be found around the seashore, gorging on fish.

► *Nyctosaurus* This reptile eats fish too, but you might find it by the river.

◄ *Archaeopteryx* Try searching in a wooded area for this early bird.

◄ *Quetzalcoatlus* This giant flying monster is so big it could fly anywhere on the island! But you hope to have a glimpse of it from the wide plains.

FLYING MONSTER SAFARI

You're going to need wings of your own to get as close as you dare to the pterosaurs ('winged lizards'). So you take to the air in a microlight – a small, open plane.

You will need to be careful flying around the mountainous island. The unpredictable air currents can be as dangerous as the flying reptiles.

You will be flying alongside giants that have wingspans the size of fighter jets, and snapping jaws that could swallow you whole.

SAFARI ESSENTIALS

Protective clothing A pilot helmet for flight is essential. You also have claw-proof clothing for when you track pterosaurs at ground level.

Video camera You can fix this camera to the cockpit of the microlight to record the flying creatures in mid-air.

dinoPad Your special e-book reader holds all information known about prehistoric animals, including these awesome flying creatures.

FLYING FISHERS

You approach the island at a steady speed. Suddenly, you aren't alone: three pterosaurs like beaked dragons surround the microlight and seem to guide you into their ominous world. You recognize the distinctive shape of the *Pteranodons'* heads. Each waft of their giant wings nearly sends your craft off course, so you take a dive to escape.

Pteranodon's huge wings are made up of leathery membranes supported by muscles and bones.

Monster-size *Pteranodon* have a wingspan of up to 30 ft (9 m) — that's as wide as your microlight.

Some *Pteranodon* have long crests. Perhaps they act as rudders in flight, or balance the weight of their long jaws.

The *Pteranodon's* head is longer than its body, with long, toothless jaws for catching fish.

Pteranodon has featured in many movies, including *Jurassic Park III.*

Meaning of name: Toothless wing
Size: 30 ft (9 m) wingspan
Family: Pteranodontidae
Period: Late Cretaceous
Weight: 20–30 lb (9–14 kg)
Found in: North America
Diet: Fish

FACT AND FICTION

▼ **Snapping beaks** Unlike those shown in many movies, real *Pteranodon* have no teeth. However, if a *Pteranodon* mistook you for a fish, it could eat most of you in one gulp with its 4 ft- (1.2 m-) long jaws.

▶ **Grabbing claws** Movies that show human beings being carried away in the claws of *Pteranodon* are not based on evidence. The *Pteranodon's* rear claws are not strong enough to carry a human!

▼ **Crest shapes** *Pteranodon* are nearly always shown with long crests on their heads. However, the sizes and shapes of fossilized crests vary greatly.

LITTLE MONSTERS

As you dive and the *Pteranodon* leave, you hit a cloud of buzzing, biting insects. Worse still, the insects are prey to a flock of seagull-sized *Anurognathus,* which soon flap around your head, obscuring the view through your visor. Your helmet protects your head but an *Anurognathus* nips your neck. While hardly able to see, you must attempt a landing...

Anurognathus has very strong jaws for feeding on insects while in flight.

Meaning of name: Frog jaw
Size: 20 in (50 cm) wingspan
Family: Anurognathidea
Period: Late Jurassic
Weight: 3–6 oz (80–160 g)
Found in: Europe
Diet: Insects

Anurognathus' tail is short so that it doesn't get in the way while the creature hunts for insects like beetles and flies.

TINY TERRORS

▼ **Anurognathus** is in the first group of pterosaurs to evolve, the rhamphorhynchoids. These creatures are often small. Some of them feed on the insects buzzing around dinosaurs' heads.

Anurognathus are warm-blooded and covered in fur.

▶ **Jeholopterus** may suck the blood from dinosaurs. It has two vampire-like fangs to pierce the skin, a wide-opening mouth, and clasping hands.

▼ **Sordes** has 0.25 in (6 mm) hairs all over its body. If it needs a coat to keep warm, it must be warm-blooded.

Anurognathus means 'frog jaw' and its wide, frog-like mouth is useful as a scoop for snatching insects in flight.

45

FLYING MACHINES

You land on bumpy ground, and taxi to a halt near a riverside. You grab your camera as you leave the plane, ready to film an incredible gathering. A flock of *Eudimorphodon* is snapping up fish. You gasp at their amazing flying skills, but on the ground they are clumsy and can hardly walk. Suddenly they all panic – there are splashes and squawks. What has startled them?

Rhamphorhynchoids like *Eudimorphodon* are clumsy on land. They drag their huge wings, and their long tails get in the way.

The stiff tail has a rudder-like end, perhaps used to help steer when flying.

The legs are strong enough to survive the heavy landing of its body and big wings.

Eudimorphodon is one of the earliest living pterosaurs known.

Meaning of name: True two-formed tooth
Size: 3 ft (1 m) wingspan
Family: Campylognathoididae
Period: Late Triassic
Weight: 2 lb (1 kg)
Found in: Europe
Diet: Fish

MASTERS OF THE SKY

The earliest pterosaurs were gliders. *Eudimorphodon* was among the first to master true flight.

▶ Some pterosaurs use their feet to hang from trees and to take off from branches or cliff faces.

▶ Although pterosaurs are bat-like in many ways, they have more control over their wings than bats, and are more stable fliers.

There are more than a hundred teeth in the mouth of a *Eudimorphodon*. There are fangs near the front — perfect for grabbing slippery fish.

◀ Many pterosaurs prey on fish. They are able to dive down and take a bite from the sea without free-falling.

SAIL HEADS

The flock of *Eudimorphodon* scatter at the sight of this majestic monster – a *Nyctosaurus*. The sail on its head is as big as a yacht's. As you film it nervously, you wonder why it has such a huge crest. Perhaps it's just there to impress – it certainly scared off the competition. Now it has the river fish to itself.

With a wingspan of up to 10 ft (3 m), *Nyctosaurus* cruises low over the water at a speed of about 20 mph (35 km/h).

The antler-like bone struts in the sail are up to three times the length of the skull.

Unlike most pterosaurs, *Nyctosaurus* does not have claws that can grasp, so it can't land on a tree or cling to a cliff.

Nyctosaurus has crest bones similar in length to its wings.

Meaning of name: Night lizard
Size: 10 ft (3 m) wingspan
Family: Nyctosauridea
Period: Late Cretaceous
Weight: 11–22 lb (5–10 kg)
Found in: North and South America
Diet: Fish

GIANT CRESTS

▶ No evidence exists of there being a membrane across the bones of the *Nyctosaurus'* headcrest. Without a membrane, it would look like this. Some *Nyctosaurus* without crest bones have also been found.

▼ The *Thalassodromeus'* ('sea runner') sail makes up three-quarters of its 4 ft 8 in- (1.4 m-) long skull. Perhaps the sail helps regulate its body heat, like a solar panel or car radiator, as it skims the water looking for fish.

The tip of its mouth is needle-sharp, so it can easily skewer fish.

▼ The *Pteranodon* crest consists of one solid bone, strong enough to act as an air brake if it turns its head to one side.

NEEDLE TEETH

There's an ear-splitting squawk – you spin round to see a pterosaur nearly twice as big as the *Nyctosaurus*. It's a *Cearadactylus*! You lie flat as it dives towards the river. Your hands are shaking, but you keep the camera running. There's just time to capture those needle-sharp teeth and crocodile-like jaws. Then it swoops straight at you! You run for shelter.

Cearadactylus' wingspan is at least three times your height.

Cearadactylus has long jaws like a crocodile's, which suggests it ate fish.

Meaning of name: Ceará finger (Ceará is a Brazilian state.)
Size: 20 ft (6 m) wingspan
Family: Ornithocheiridae
Period: Middle Cretaceous
Weight: 30–40 lb (14–18 kg)
Found in: South America
Diet: Fish

Like many pterosaurs, *Cearadactylus* lays eggs.

CRUSHERS AND SCOOPERS

Even the largest pterosaurs are not much heavier than the largest birds alive today. They have hollow bones only about 0.04 in (1 mm) thick.

▼ *Dsungaripterus* has a narrow, upward-pointing beak for opening shellfish, and bony knobs instead of teeth act as shell and bone crushers.

▼ *Pterodaustro* is like a flamingo, scooping and filtering its food using a large beak. The lower jaw has brush-like bristles that work like a sieve.

Cearadactylus' jaws have small interlocking teeth, with a cage of longer teeth at the front to stop fish slipping away.

51

EARLY BIRDS

You keep running until you reach the safety of a forest. There's a rustle amongst the trees – you jump, then laugh, as a strange turkey-like creature flutters down from a branch and lands heavily at your feet. It looks at you before flapping off. You can hardly believe it. You've just seen one of the first birds – the *Archaeopteryx*! You follow it, leaving your microlight far behind...

Weak flight muscles mean it cannot fly as well as a pterosaur. It flutters short distances, walks on the ground and perches on branches while hunting for insects to eat.

Archaeopteryx has the wings and feathers of a modern bird and is believed to have been the first bird to exist.

IS IT A BIRD?
NO, IT'S A DINOSAUR

▼ **Compsognathus** has a bird-like build and is the size of a chicken, but it is a dinosaur. It may have been covered with feathers. Feathered dinosaurs are sometimes called dino-birds.

Archaeopteryx is a primitive bird. It is thought to be the link between dinosaurs and modern-day birds.

Meaning of name: Ancient wing
Size: 1 ft 6 in (50 cm) wingspan
Family: Archaeopterygidae
Period: Late Jurassic
Weight: Up to 2.2 lb (1 kg)
Found in: Germany
Diet: Insects

▶ **Scansoriopteryx** is a feathered, sparrow-sized, tree-dwelling dinosaur. It has a very long third finger for getting insects out of tree holes.

▼ **Caudipteryx**, like other dino-birds, cannot fly. It probably wades in lakes and perches on branches.

Dinosaur features (a long, stiff, bony tail, three-clawed hands and jaws with teeth) show it evolved from the dinosaurs, not the pterosaurs.

LIZARD GLIDERS

As you run through the trees after the *Archaeopteryx*, a rough wing suddenly brushes past your face, followed by the whiplash of a tail that burns your cheek. It's a *Coelurosauravus* – a gliding lizard! More creatures appear, forming a flapping mass around you. You're not feeling welcome here – it's time to get out of the forest. But you're lost, and where's the microlight?

Coelurosauravus is one of the oldest flying reptiles.

More than 20 hollow bones and skin form a web-like wing. The wings close for protection when it lands.

A long tail helps with stability as it glides and snaps up insects in the air.

OLD TIMERS

Coelurosauravus **is the earliest known gliding vertebrate.**

Meaning of name: Flying hollow lizard
Length: 1 ft (30 cm)
Family: Coelurosauravidae
Period: Permian
Weight: Unknown
Found in: Madagascar, Germany, England
Diet: Insects

▼ The earliest creatures to fly were insects, like *Meganeura* – a giant dragonfly as big as a parrot. *Meganeura* buzzed around prehistoric Carboniferous forests.

▼ Fossil evidence shows that *Meganeura*'s wingspan stretched an astonishing 2 ft 6 in (75 cm). Some scientists believe that insects were able to grow larger in the Carboniferous period because there was more oxygen in the air.

Streamlined *Coelurosauravus* can easily glide hundreds of feet from tree to tree.

PUNK PTEROSAUR

You reach a clearing and look up into the sky. Against the bright sunlight you see the biggest pterosaur so far – the *Tapejara*. Its sharp and turned-down beak looks capable of biting off your head. The huge crest looks like a Mohican. Trembling as you film it, you wish your microlight was within sight, ready for a quick escape. You set off again, feeling more and more lost in this threatening place.

Tapejara has a tall crest, the purpose of which is still a mystery.

Meaning of name: Old being
Size: 12 ft (3.6 m) wingspan
Family: Tapejaridae
Period: Cretaceous
Weight: 80 lb (36 kg)
Found in: South America
Diet: Fish

The wingspan is nearly three times the height of an adult human: 16 ft (5 m). Its head alone is 3 ft (1 m) tall.

The large crest is made up of a membrane stretched between two struts of bone. It might be used for display or for steering, like the sail on a yacht.

HEAD AND BEAK CRESTS

▼ Some pterosaurs, such as *Tropeognathus*, had crests on their beaks, not their heads. Crests on the lower and upper jaw perhaps helped it cut through the surface of the water as it flew low, skimming the water to catch fish.

▼ The many blood vessels in *Tupuxara*'s crest may allow it to change its appearance according to the creature's mood, just as anger might redden a human face.

Tapejara's strong beak can bite into fruit, catch fish or feed on carrion.

◄ Perhaps only male pterosaurs have showy crests. Female pterosaur fossils have been found without crests, when males of the same species have them.

SEASIDE FLOCK

You reach the edge of the forest and discover not a river but a beach, crowded with a flock of noisy *Dimorphodons*. You get excellent shots of the *Dimorphodons* taking off, landing and stumbling across the rocks. Then you spot some eggs in the sand. One starts to crack... then the video screen goes blank. You've got to get back to the microlight for another battery!

The deep beak has 30 to 40 sharp pointed teeth in each jaw and is an excellent fish-catching weapon.

Perhaps *Dimorphodon's* beak becomes brighter during the breeding season to attract a mate.

Claws on both the feet and hands make it easy to cling to cliff faces.

The first fossil remains of *Dimorphodon* were found by Mary Anning in England in 1828.

Meaning of name: Two-formed tooth
Size: 4 ft (1.3 m) wingspan
Family: Dimorphodontidae
Period: Jurassic
Weight: 5 lb (2.3 kg)
Found in: Europe, Central America
Diet: Fish, insects, perhaps small vertebrates and carrion

CRAWLERS AND POLE-VAULTERS

Scientists used to think that *Dimorphodon* walked on two legs, but this is now seen as improbable – they were likely to fall over!

▼ It is more likely that, like other pterosaurs, *Dimophordon* leaned forward and crawled along on its two legs and two wings.

▼ For take-off, *Dimophordon* pushed off its back legs and used its wings for extra leverage – just as a pole-vaulter pushes him or herself higher with a pole.

Fish-eating birds like *Dimorphodon* may have formed nest-making colonies on cliff edges, or buried their eggs in the sand, like turtles.

THE PLUMED SERPENT

You find the river and follow its course back to the microlight. Just as you change the battery in your camera, the sky turns black. Is it a storm cloud? No, it's the most awesome thing you've seen in your life, the largest flying creature the world has known – *Quetzalcoatlus*! You jump into the microlight and join it in the sky, but you don't spot the open jaws you're heading towards...

Quetzalcoatlus flies effortlessly, hardly flapping its wings. It uses air currents to carry its weight.

Its 35 ft (10.5 m) wingspan, small body weight and shape mean it can fly up to 80 mph (130 km/h) for seven to ten days.

The long-necked *Quetzalcoatlus* is the largest-ever flying creature known to exist.

Meaning of name: Named after the Mesoamerican god Quetzalcoatl
Size: 30 ft (9 m) wingspan
Family: Azhdarchidae
Period: Late Cretaceous
Weight: 200 lb (91 kg)
Found in: North America
Diet: Fish and meat

Its flight range could be as far as 12,000 miles (19,300 km) – that's half way around the world!

SKY-GOD

▼ *Quetzalcoatlus* is named after the sky-god Quetzalcoatl – a mythical plumed serpent, worshipped by Middle American peoples such as the Aztecs and Toltecs.

▼ Like a modern stork, *Quetzalcoatlus* may have not only eaten fish, but spent time on the ground scavenging for carrion, or eating worms and insects. It might even have preyed on small dinosaurs.

61

MIGRATION

Just in time, you roll the microlight and escape the toothy jaws of an *Ornithocheirus*. But then you realize you're right in the middle of a migratory flight path! Each flap of an *Ornithocheirus* wing nearly sends your craft into a spin. One gets too close – one tear to its wing and the magnificent creature will fall. Horrified, you feel like an invader in their world; you're a danger to them. It's time to fly back to the ship.

Pterosaur lungs are attached to air sacs in other parts of their bodies. Air sacs in the wings may help to keep the shape of the wings, and to maintain stability during flight.

The 'keel' shape at the end of the beak has numerous possible uses: to smash open shellfish, to frighten off rivals or to attract a mate.

Some fossils of *Ornithocheirus* have been found with round boney crests at the tips of its upper and lower jaws.

Meaning of name: Bird hand
Size: 10–20 ft (3–6 m) wingspan
Family: Ornithocheiridae
Period: Middle Cretaceous
Weight: 50–100 lb (23–46 kg)
Found in: Western Europe, South America
Diet: Fish

Pterosaur wings are vulnerable — more so than the resilient feather covering of the first dino-birds and the birds of today.

FOSSIL PUZZLES

▼ Putting together bits of fossilized bones to make an identifiable pterosaur can be difficult, even impossible. So many fossil fragments of *Ornithocheirus* have been found that scientists have grouped them into 40 different species, without a complete skeleton of any of them!

▼ Scientist agree that pterosaurs, including *Ornithocheirus*, have been extinct for 65 million years. However, some people claim to have seen a flying animal like a pterosaur around Papua New Guinea. They call it the ropen. Perhaps it is a living fossil.

FLYING MONSTER REPORT

Back at the ship, you meet with the paleontologists on your support team. They are fascinated by the videos you have taken and together you prepare a presentation for the public, starring the vast wings of *Quetzalcoatlus*.

Some of the most terrifying pterosaurs were not the biggest on your safari. Years later, your blood still runs cold when you recall the flock of tiny *Anurognathus* that fluttered around your head – and you will always bear the vampire-like scar from the one that bit your neck.

Quetzalcoatlus – 36 ft (11 m)
Pteranodon – 30 ft (9 m)
Cearadactylus – 20 ft (6 m)
Tapejara – 12 ft (3.6 m)
Nyctosaurus – 10 ft (3 m)

Dimorphodon – 4 ft (1.3 m)
Eudimorphodon – 3 ft (1 m)
Anurognathus – 1 ft 6 in (50 cm)
Archaeopteryx – 1 ft 6 in (50 cm)
Coelurosauravus – 1 ft (30 cm)

The creatures you saw on safari originally lived at different times throughout prehistory. This chart shows the different periods in which they lived. MYA stands for million years ago.

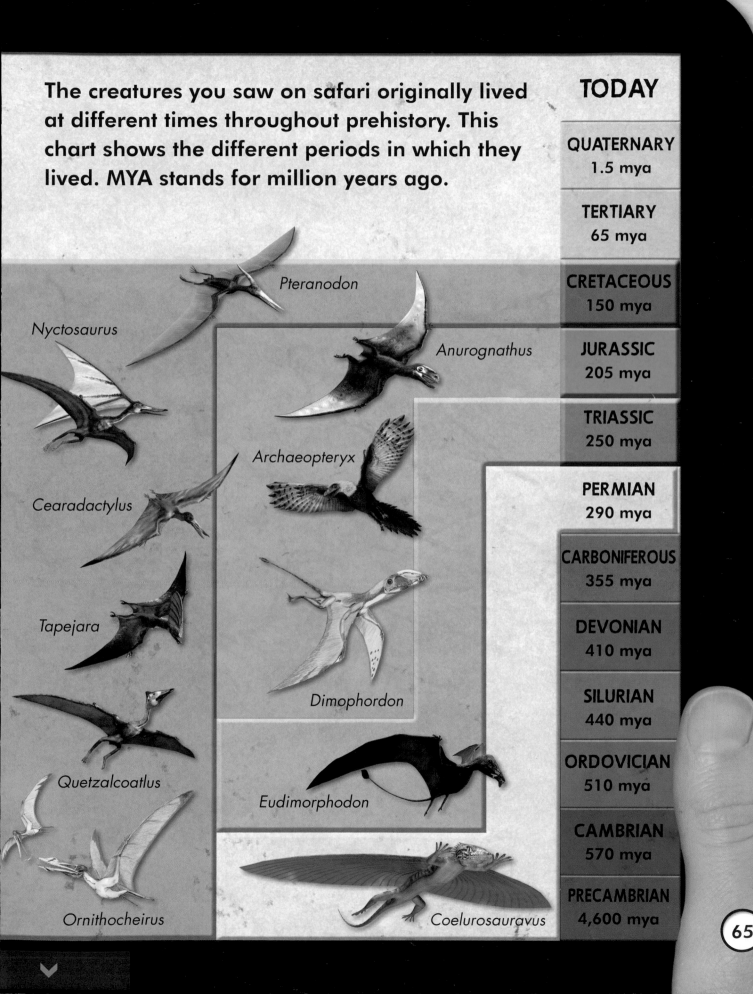

Pteranodon

Nyctosaurus

Anurognathus

Archaeopteryx

Cearadactylus

Tapejara

Dimophordon

Quetzalcoatlus

Eudimorphodon

Ornithocheirus

Coelurosauravus

TODAY

| QUATERNARY |
| 1.5 mya |

| TERTIARY |
| 65 mya |

| CRETACEOUS |
| 150 mya |

| JURASSIC |
| 205 mya |

| TRIASSIC |
| 250 mya |

| PERMIAN |
| 290 mya |

| CARBONIFEROUS |
| 355 mya |

| DEVONIAN |
| 410 mya |

| SILURIAN |
| 440 mya |

| ORDOVICIAN |
| 510 mya |

| CAMBRIAN |
| 570 mya |

| PRECAMBRIAN |
| 4,600 mya |

SEA MONSTERS

Are you ready to journey into a terrifying undersea world? Today your safari takes you to the oceans surrounding the secret dinosaur islands. Reports suggest that prehistoric predators still swim here. Your mission is to photograph such horrors as ancient sharks, giant sea scorpions and monstrous reptiles.

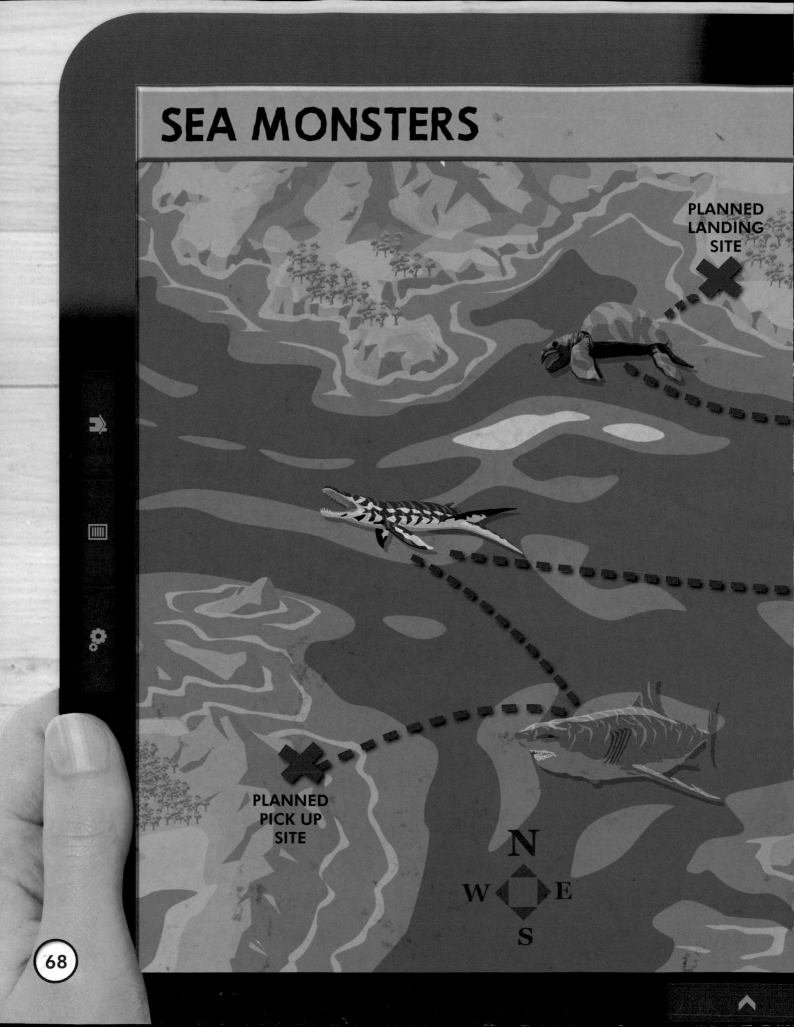

SEA MONSTERS

PLANNED
LANDING
SITE

PLANNED
PICK UP
SITE

N
W E
S

You check your map one last time before you set out.

DINOSAURS TO SPOT

▶ **Archelon** is an ancient turtle that hunts jellyfish in the shallow waters.

◀ **Xiphactinus** travels in schools, eating up smaller fish in the shallows.

▶ **Plesiosaurus** lurks in the medium depth waters, deep enough for it to swim but shallow enough for it to breathe at the surface.

▲ **Liopleurodon** is the largest flesh-eating vertebrate ever. You will find it in deeper waters.

◀ **Megalodon** is a gigantic shark. It lives in very deep water where it preys on everything, even whales.

SEA MONSTER SAFARI

You plan to use scuba gear to explore shallow waters. You will use a submersible to view deeper, more dangerous areas. You hope that the submersible is strong enough to withstand attacks from giant prehistoric sharks and meat-eating reptiles!

More than anything, you hope that you will see a creature nicknamed the 'Monster'. The deadly *Liopleurodon* is the *Tyrannosaurus rex* of the sea!

SAFARI ESSENTIALS

Scuba equipment Your scuba-diving equipment includes a shark deterrent shield, which uses a small electric field to keep predators away.

Camera This hand-held underwater camera is for your scuba dives. The submersible also has a video camera fitted.

dinoPad Your waterproof prehistoric e-book reader will be very useful – all known information on underwater prehistoric life has been uploaded.

GIANT SNAILS

After checking your scuba equipment, you make your first dive. Below the surface, you're amazed to see living ammonites. And one that is as big as a tractor wheel is heading right for you. Frozen with horror, you wait to be crushed... but it just cruises past, its tentacles touching your face. It's being pursued by something much scarier.

This ammonite has a spiral shell. The creature lives in the largest, outermost chamber of the spiral. As it grows bigger, it adds another larger chamber to live in.

By shooting out water from a funnel-shaped opening, the ammonite propels itself through the sea.

Ammonite shells range from less than 0.4 in (1 cm) to 6.5 ft (2 m). The shells house slug-like creatures with tentacles; some 'slugs' are at least twice as long as you are tall.

THE EVIDENCE

Fossils are the evidence we have that proves the existence of prehistoric wonders like the ammonites.

◄ **An ammonite fossil** forms after the creature dies and decays on the seabed. A hollow showing the shell's shape is left behind. Sometimes the hollow fills up with sediment that hardens into a fossil.

Ammonites are closely related to modern-day squids and octopuses.

Meaning of name: Named after Amun, an ancient Egyptian god who had rams' horns
Size: 0.4 in (1 cm) to 6.5 ft (2 m) diameter
Family: Cephalopoda
Period: Triassic to Cretaceous
Found: Commonly found in Cretaceous rocks all around the world
Diet: Plankton (tiny plants and animals)

► **A cross-section of an ammonite shell** shows the chambers inside. By squirting the seawater out of some chambers, the ammonite can make itself more or less buoyant (floating higher or lower).

◄ **The pearly nautilus** is the only known living relative of the prehistoric ammonite.

TERRIFYING TURTLES

The ammonites are fleeing from two giant turtles – each the size of a car. These *Archelon* hungrily graze on jellyfish, then snap at ammonites that are too slow to escape. You bravely take photos. But soon, the only food left is you! You get the shark deterrent shield ready but fumble, and it slips from your hands. Then, out of the gloom, comes an unlikely rescuer.

Archelon is a marine turtle – the largest turtle ever to exist.

Meaning of name: Ruling turtle
Size: Around 13 ft (4 m) long
Family: Protostegidae
Period: Late Cretaceous
Weight: 2.5 tons (2,200 kg)
Found in: USA
Diet: Plankton, small sea creatures

The *Archelon's* lightweight shell and strong flippers allow it to swim long distances into the open sea.

Like today's leatherback turtles, *Archelon* struggles up onto the beach to lay its eggs in the sand. It does this at night, in the hope that it won't be spotted by a hungry dinosaur.

GIANTS OF THE TURTLE WORLD

◄ The giant *Archelon* is omnivorous. As well as eating jellyfish, squid and carrion, it also feeds on plants such as seaweed.

► The broad crushing surfaces of an *Archelon* beak can also crack open giant prehistoric shells, such as a 4 ft- (1.2 m-) wide clam's shell.

▼ The first, 11 ft- (3.4 m-) long, *Archelon* specimen was found back in 1895. An even bigger one was found in 1970 at 13 ft (4 m) long! The *Archelon* holds the record as the largest turtle to have lived.

Its shell is leathery, rather than hard like a modern-day turtle's.

DEADLY JAWS

The water froths as a sea reptile the size of a bus bursts into view, ramming the end of its snout right into an *Archelon*. The stunned turtle is soon trapped between its jaws. With a sideways thrust of the tail, the *Tylosaurus* carries off its meal. More *Tylosaurus* appear, snapping up ammonites. Horrified by this feeding frenzy, you swim away – it's time to seek the safety of your submersible.

The *Tylosaurus* has pointed, cone-shaped teeth for seizing, tearing and crushing. Two extra rows of teeth on the roof of its mouth help to keep a firm hold on its prey.

Tylosaurus is the largest of the mosasaurs, a group of fast-swimming prehistoric sea reptiles.

Meaning of name: Lump lizard
Size: 40 ft (12 m) long
Family: Mosasauridae
Period: Late Cretaceous
Found in: USA
Diet: Fish, ammonites, reptiles

Like other mosasaurs, the *Tylosaurus* has lizard-like scales.

Mosasaurs feed on ammonites, turtles, birds and even fast-moving giants, such as sharks and plesiosaurs.

SWIMMING LIZARDS

◄ *Tylosaurus*'s name, which means 'lump lizard', refers to the rounded shape of the end of its nose. Combined with high-speed swimming, the nose makes an excellent battering ram.

▲ *Tylosaurus*'s powerful tail is flattened rather than rounded. This helps the creature to push its body fast through the water. A quick burst of speed is useful for a surprise attack.

► Mosasaurs have snake-like jaws that open extra wide so that they can swallow smaller prey whole.

DEMON FISH

Between you and the submersible is a school of hideous fish. These huge, bony creatures, 16 feet (5 m) in length, are chasing smaller fish at top speed. You swim on, hoping that they won't take a sudden interest in you – you could lose both your legs from a single *Xiphactinus* bite. You clamber into the submersible, sigh with relief, and lock the hatch firmly behind you.

A powerful tail gives this fast-moving predator a top speed of 37 mph (60 km/h).

Xiphactinus has camouflage markings so that it can hide and ambush its prey.

Xiphactinus is often described as one of the most aggressive bony fish.

Meaning of name: Sword-ray
Size: 15–20 ft (4.5–6 m) long
Family: Ichthyodectidae
Period: Late Cretaceous
Found in: North America, Europe, Australia, Canada
Diet: Fish and other marine life

DEADLY JAWS

▶ Unlike the jawless fish living alongside them, bony fish are able to bite into their prey and grip them in their mouths. *Xiphactinus* has a lethal, upturned jaw and fang-like teeth.

▲ *Dunkleosteus* has slicing bony plates instead of teeth, and a plated body for protection. It can easily attack and kill a prehistoric shark like *Stethacanthus*.

▲ *Coelacanth* was thought to have become extinct, like *Xiphactinus*, at the end of the Cretaceous period. But a living *Coelacanth* was discovered in South Africa in 1938!

Xiphactinus is both the predator and prey of sharks, depending on their size.

LONG-NECKED SWIMMERS

Safely back in the submersible, you catch a glimpse of a long-necked creature, and set off in pursuit. You watch the *Plesiosaurus* swim, curving its body like a seal. The video camera records its sharp teeth snapping together around a fish like a trap. Now and then it lifts its head above the surface to breathe. After more photos, you take the submersible deeper, seeking the 'Monster'.

Plesiosaurus is a type of plesiosaur, which along with the ichthyosaurs, dominated the Jurassic seas.

Meaning of name: Almost a lizard
Size: 11 ft (3.5 m) long
Family: Plesiosauroidea
Period: Early Jurassic
Found in: England
Diet: Fish and other marine life

The first *Plesiosaurus* to be studied was described as a 'snake threaded through the body of a turtle' because of its long neck and tail.

THE LOCH NESS PLESIOSAUR?

▶ Some people believe that a large plesiosaur-like monster lives in the deep waters of Loch Ness, in Scotland. This photo, taken in 1934, turned out to be a hoax.

The long, sharp teeth interlock when the jaws close, to make a cage in which fish can be trapped.

▼ Another hoaxer claimed that footprints were found on the shore of the loch. These were actually made using a hippopotamus-foot umbrella stand.

▼ Many people say they've seen the Loch Ness monster. Some descriptions do sound like a plesiosaur: supposedly it has a long neck and small head, and comes to the surface to breathe.

The front paddles keep the creature stable. The back limbs push its body through the water.

SHARKS ON PATROL

Suddenly, shadows darken your way. You slow the engines of the submersible as two sharks swim dangerously close. You photograph their greedy mouths. Using the dinoPad, you identify them as *Stethacanthus*. Their strange, anvil-shaped dorsal fins show they are males. One thumps its head against the glass. Terrified the glass will shatter, you dive deeper into the darkness.

Stethacanthus may migrate long distances, returning to the same waters each year to mate and give birth.

Sharks are survivors. They are over 400 million years old and have lived through at least five mass extinctions.

Stethacanthus is a smallish shark, noted for the male's anvil-shaped dorsal fin.

Meaning of name: Chest spike
Size: 2 ft 4 in to 6 ft (70 cm to 2 m) long
Family: Stethacanthidae
Period: Late Devonian–Cretaceous
Found in: Europe, North America
Diet: Fish and other marine life

ANVIL HEADS

► Some scientists think that *Stethacanthus'* head bristles are meant to look like teeth in a giant hungry mouth, which might scare off attackers.

◄ Only males have been found with anvil-shaped dorsal fins. Perhaps they were used for showing off their power and strength during courtship with females.

▼ Fossil coprolites (prehistoric animal droppings) can tell us about ancient sharks' diets. We know that *Stethacanthus'* diet includes small fish and ammonites.

Brush-like scales stick up from the top of the head of *Stethacanthus* and the top of the dorsal fin. No-one is certain what they are for.

FISH-LIZARDS

It's pitch black as you reach the ocean bed. You swivel the searchlight and there's a sight that makes you smile. You've seen so many ichthyosaur fossils – but this one is very much alive! It's the biggest ichthyosaur ever to exist, the 50 feet- (15 m-) long *Shonisaurus*. While you're busy taking photos, you have no idea that something terrifying has swum up behind you...

The *Shonisaurus* is an early ichthyosaur, with a body shape similar to a whale. With this body shape, it could probably not swim very fast.

Shonisaurus may be huge, but it usually feeds on small creatures, such as squid-like belemnites.

Shonisaurus is an early ichthyosaur. Ichthyosaurs are aquatic reptiles that have a fish-like body shape.

Meaning of name: Lizard from the Shoshone Mountains
Size: 50 ft (15 m) long
Family: Shonisauridae
Period: Late Triassic
Weight: 40 tons
Found in: USA, Canada
Diet: Fish and other marine life

Ichthyosaurs have to swim to the surface to breathe — they do not have gills.

AWESOME ICHTHYOSAURS

◄ The *Shonisaurus* has the biggest eye of any known vertebrate (any animal with a backbone). Each eye socket is 3 ft (1 m) in diameter. Each giant eyeball is protected by a bony ring.

▼ The first ichthyosaur fossil (a skull) was found by a Victorian girl when she was just 12 years old. Mary Anning was poor and gathered fossils for a living. Once, she was nearly killed by a landslide when fossil hunting.

▼ This fossil of an ichthyosaur flipper clearly shows its paddle-like shape.

THE 'MONSTER'

The submersible shakes, and you grab the controls – you've been rammed! Your stomach lurches as the giant plesiosaur pushes you and your craft away. Moments later, its vicious teeth tear into the ichthyosaur's flesh. It's a *Liopleurodon*, the 'Monster' you've been searching for! You are delighted at last to capture your prize on film.

At twice the length of a killer whale, *Liopleurodon* is the largest flesh-eating vertebrate ever found.

Its cucumber-sized teeth (the same size as those of a *Tyrannosaurus rex*) have deep roots, giving it a very strong bite.

Liopleurodon is a large marine reptile and the biggest of the plesiosaurs.

Meaning of name: Smooth-sided teeth
Size: Possibly up to 80 ft (25 m) long
Family: Pliosauridae
Period: Mid Jurassic
Found in: Europe, Russia
Diet: Fish and other marine life

It uses its 10 ft-(3 m-) long paddles like wings to 'fly' through the water.

TYRANT OF THE SEA

▼ *Liopleurodon* and *Tyrannosaurus rex* are both considered giant predators, but the tyrant of the sea is almost double the length of *T. rex*.

▼ Using their limbs like oars, which they wave vertically, plesiosaurs virtually fly through the water. With extra effort from their back limbs, they can probably swim at about 6 mph (10 km/h).

◀ Plesiosaurs swallow stones to help grind down food and to act like the ballast in a ship. Stones in their lower abdomen give extra stability.

DEADLY SCORPION

As you reach the coral reef, the submersible comes to a juddering halt. Something is caught in the motor! You swim out to fix the problem. An insect-like creature crawls stealthily towards you, flexing its pincer-like claws. It's a *Pterygotus*, a sea scorpion more than 7 feet (2 m) long. Then suddenly, it swims off, flapping its paddle-like limbs in a panic. What has scared it so much?

Pterygotus has two pairs of eyes — a small, upward-facing pair on top of its head, and two large eyes near the front.

Pterygotus has two wider limbs to use as paddles for swimming.

Pterygotus can ambush its prey by lying hidden in the sand, with just its eyes peering out.

> *Pterygotus* is the second largest sea scorpion (eurypterid) and a top predator in the Silurian and Devonian seas.
>
> **Meaning of name:** Wing-animal or finned one
> **Size:** 7 ft 7 in (2.3 m)
> **Family:** Pterygotidae
> **Period:** Late Silurian—early Devonian
> **Found in:** All continents except Antarctica
> **Diet:** Fish, trilobites, other marine animals

Pterygotus has strong jaws and a hard, protective exoskeleton.

MORE UNDERSEA HORRORS

▼ The giant squid-like *Orthocone* grows up to 36 ft (11 m) long and feeds on sea scorpions and fish. It can trap the biggest of sea scorpions with its tentacles, then pull it into its mouth.

▶ Trilobites scurry around the sea floor like woodlice. They swim upside down. Trilobites have a hard outer covering for protection, and some also have dangerous-looking spikes and spines.

▼ The biggest sea scorpion is the *Jaekelopterus rhenaniae*. At 8 ft (2.5 m), it's the size of a crocodile, so you wouldn't want to get too close!

TERROR SHARK

Two incredible creatures pass alongside the submersible. A vast prehistoric shark is pursuing a huge whale. You climb back into the craft, so that you can film the encounter. The shark grabs the flipper of the whale to disable it – and a violent struggle follows. You're suddenly thrown from your seat, as the 50-ton body of the shark hits your craft. A crack appears in the glass and water begins to trickle through.

Megalodon's jaws open wide enough for a person to stand upright between them.

Megalodon waits for whales to head to the surface to breathe, so that it can attack from below. The whale has nowhere to escape.

Megalodon is two to three times bigger than today's great white shark. From 25 to 1.6 million years ago *Megalodon* was the top ocean predator – no other predator was powerful enough to attack it.

SO MANY TEETH

▶ *Megalodon* has more teeth than you may imagine – 276! They line the jaws in three to five rows. The front rows are used to catch prey. The others take their place as they wear out.

▼ *Helicoprion*, a shark that lived about 290 million years ago, has a spiral of teeth. No one knows for sure where they were positioned, but perhaps they were in the lower jaw. Wherever they were, they would make an efficient slicing machine.

▼ The biggest fossil teeth ever found come from a whale (*Livyatan melvillei*) that lived 12–13 million years ago. They are 14 in (36 cm) long!

SNAKE NECK

The water inside the damaged submersible is already up to your waist, and you only just manage to pilot it to your anchored boat. As you set off home, you get to film your last safari surprise: these awesome shore-living reptiles, *Tanystropheus*. You watch amazed as one whips its neck around to snap up a fish.

Tanystropheus walks in shallow waters, then stretches its neck out like a fishing line to catch fish or ammonites.

Its long neck isn't very flexible, but it is incredibly long — 10 ft (3 m) in all.

Tanystropheus is a shore-living sea reptile related to snakes, lizards and crocodiles.

Meaning of name: Long strap
Size: 20 ft (6 m) long
Family: Tanystropidae
Period: Middle to late Triassic
Found in: Europe, Middle East and China
Diet: Fish, other marine life, insects

Powerful rear leg muscles allow it to lean back and so stretch up its head.

AMAZING ANATOMY

► *Tanystropheus'* tail can snap off if grabbed by a predator. This is a good way of escaping, and the tail will grow back.

► The teeth in the jaw of *Tanystropheus* vary according to its age: the young have teeth suitable for eating insects; the adults have interlocking teeth for eating fish.

► The neck is completely out of proportion with the rest of the body. As a counterweight (a weight for balance), there are extra muscles at the back of the body, behind the hips.

SEA MONSTER SAFARI REPORT

Back on the ship, you write a report and review the footage. Some scientists want to make a documentary about the sea monsters and it looks like you have more than enough excellent shots to do it. Your own blood still runs cold when you recall *Liopleurodon* ramming your submersible!

The most awesome thing about the sea creatures you saw during your dives was their incredible size – shells the size of tractor wheels, turtles as big as cars, and sharks with teeth as long as your arm.

■ Megalodon - 52 ft (16 m) long
■ Shonisaurus - 50 ft (15 m) long
■ Tylosaurus - 40 ft (12 m) long
■ Tanystropheus - 20 ft (6 m) long
■ Xiphactinus - 15–20 ft (5–6 m) long
■ Liopleurodon - 80 ft (25 m) long

■ Archelon - 13 ft (4 m) long
■ Plesiosaurus - 11 ft (3.5 m) long
■ Stethacanthus - 6 ft (2 m) long
■ Pterygotus - 7 ft 7 in (2.3 m)
■ Ammonite - 0.4 in (1 cm) to 6.5 ft (2 m) diameter

You plot the creatures you saw on a timeline and realize they lived at different times over a period of nearly 400 million years. In this chart, MYA stands for million years ago.

Megalodon

Ammonites

Plesiosaurus

Archelon

Xiphactinus

Liopleurodon

Tanystropheus

Shonisaurus

Tylosaurus

Stethacanthus

Pterygotus

TODAY

QUATERNARY
1.5 mya

TERTIARY
65 mya

CRETACEOUS
150 mya

JURASSIC
205 mya

TRIASSIC
250 mya

PERMIAN
290 mya

CARBONIFEROUS
355 mya

DEVONIAN
410 mya

SILURIAN
440 mya

ORDOVICIAN
510 mya

CAMBRIAN
570 mya

PRECAMBRIAN
4,600 mya

KILLER DINOSAURS

For the final two days of your dinosaur safari, you will be hunting the ferocious meat eaters of the most dangerous secret island of all – and this time you're staying the night! Getting close enough to film these hungry beasts is going to be incredibly risky!

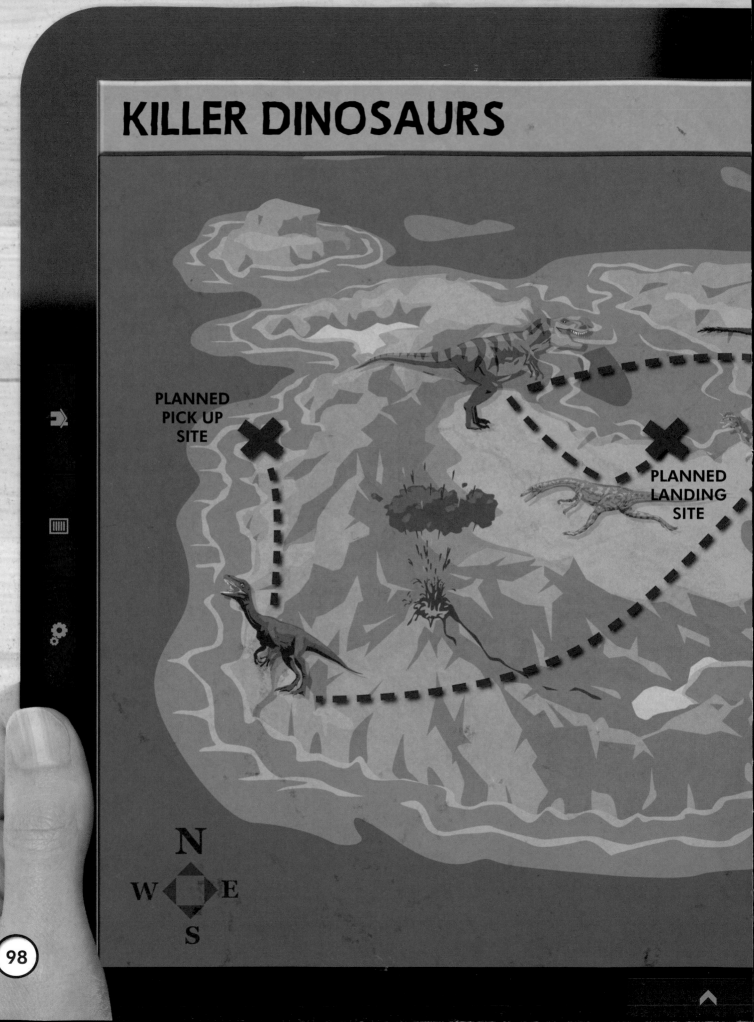

KILLER DINOSAURS

PLANNED
PICK UP
SITE

PLANNED
LANDING
SITE

N
W   E
S

You check your map one last time before you set out.

▲ **Troodon** This small, intelligent dinosaur hunts in packs on the plains.

◀ **Tyrannosaurus rex** A fearsome predator. It relies on speed to hunt herbivores on the plains.

◀ **Deinonychus** Look for packs of this raptor hunting in vegetated areas.

▲ **Dilophosaurus** This aggressive dinosaur finds prey on the grasslands.

◀ **Albertosaurus** Smaller than the T. rex, but still deadly. This predator often catches herbivores at the lake.

KILLER SAFARI

You arrive at the island by boat, which anchors off-shore. To cope with the tricky island terrain – and to make quick escapes from deadly dinosaurs – you have bought an ATV (all terrain vehicle). You drive it down a ramp, through shallow waters and across a rocky shore.

Soon you will be meeting killer dinosaurs like *Tyrannosaurus rex* – its head is nearly as long as you are tall. Beware those giant teeth. They could crush you like a bug!

SAFARI ESSENTIALS

Bones You are unlikely to need bones for bait – hungry dinosaurs will smell you out. However, a tasty bone might distract a charging killer long enough for you to escape.

Video camera As well as still shots of dinosaurs, video recordings are essential for capturing them in battle.

As you leave the beach and speed over the lush grass, you gasp at the sight of howling *Apatosaurus*.

dinoPad Your electronic reader has been updated. It contains all the latest information on killer dinosaurs, so you'll know which dinosaurs to fear the most.

SMALL BUT DEADLY

Just five minutes into your safari, you are reminded that killers come in all sizes. A herd of *Compsognathus* runs past, their bodies little bigger than chickens. You see one snap up a lizard, then run off, chewing noisily. You have barely set up your camera when something bigger suddenly looms into shot...

It stretches its flexible, long neck to catch prey between its small, sharp teeth.

The long tail helps it keep its balance as it runs.

The grasping fingers are useful for keeping a tight hold on a lizard or small mammal, ready for the first tasty bite.

Compsognathus is one of the smallest dinosaurs ever found.

Meaning of name: Pretty jaw
Height: 2 ft 4 in (0.7 m)
Length: 4 ft 7 in (1.4 m)
Family: Compsognathidae
Period: Late Cretaceous
Weight: 6.6 lb (3 kg)
Found in: France, Germany
Diet: Meat

The carnivorous (meat-eating) *Compsognathus* spends most of its time looking for small creatures to eat.

LITTLE MEAT-EATERS

Small killer dinosaurs use many different deadly hunting techniques.

▼ *Sinornithosaurus* may have grooved fangs, similar to a snake's.

▼ *Avimimus* is fast-moving and has a large brain for the size of its body, which suggests that it is capable of planning speedy surprise attacks.

▼ *Syntarsus* attacks in packs. By hunting in groups, it can bring down larger prey.

FLESH-EATING BULL

You find yourself face-to-face with a huge dinosaur – the horned *Carnotaurus*. It sniffs the air and then, as if it's caught a whiff of its prey or a competitor, it roars. Twisting its head, it glares at you. Perhaps your clothes hide the smell of your flesh because it pounds past, tracking the scent of something else. You follow from a safe distance on the ATV.

Carnotaurus' small horns are useful in a head-butting battle with a competing theropod or a fight with a rival over a mate.

It has sharp meat-tearing teeth but unusually weak jaws for a creature that needs to bite through skin and bone.

Carnotaurus is a meat-eater with unusual horns above its eyes.

Meaning of name: Meat-eating bull
Height: 9 ft 10 in (3 m)
Length: 25 ft (7.5 m)
Family: Abelisauridae
Period: Late Cretaceous
Weight: 1.1 tons (1,000 kg)
Found in: Argentina
Diet: Meat

The skin is a mass of pebble-like scales, becoming larger towards the spine. Skin impressions of nearly the entire body have given scientists an unusually clear idea of its bumpy skin.

TRACKING WITH THE SENSES

◄ The skull of the *Carnotaurus* shows it has an acute sense of smell – useful for tracking down its next live meal.

▶ Killer dinosaurs like *Carnotaurus* and *Tyrannosaurus* have simple ears – holes through which sound vibrations pass down nerve canals to the brain.

These stumpy arms are the shortest of any meat-eater.

▼ *Carnotaurus*, like other theropod dinosaurs, has forward-facing eyes. These give it binocular vision, which helps it to judge the distance of its prey.

HEAVYWEIGHTS

As you round an outcrop you come upon the *Carnotaurus'* prey: a spiky stegosaur. But another carnivore – an *Allosaurus* – is already on the scene. The *Allosaurus* tears at the plant-eater's vulnerable underbelly with its blade-like teeth. The stegosaur lashes out with its tail, but soon stumbles to the ground with exhaustion. You watch as the carnivores fight over its body.

A hungry *Allosaurus* won't be put off by the protective spikes of a stegosaur. However, it would prefer a sick or dead dinosaur that can't put up a fight.

Expandable cheeks mean that *Allosaurus* can bite off big chunks of meat to swallow whole.

Sharp serrated teeth, some twice the length of your finger, can cut through skin and flesh like a saw.

Allosaurus was at the top of the food chain in Jurassic times, and was the biggest carnivore on the planet for 10 million years.

Meaning of name: Different lizard
Height: 16 ft 6 in (5 m)
Length: 40 ft (12 m)
Family: Allosauridae
Period: Late Jurassic
Weight: 1.5 tons (1,400 kg)
Found in: North America, Australia, Tanzania
Diet: Meat

The *Huayanosaurus* is a stegosaur with an impressive array of plates and spikes.

SLOW COACHES
How fast can these big, heavy killers move?

▶ *Allosaurus* carries its huge weight on two feet. Fossils show that it often falls when running fast, so sprinting is probably used as a last option.

▼ Stegosaurs have a top speed of about 4.3 mph (7 km/h). They can't run away from theropods like the *Allosaurus*.

▶ *Allosaurus* hunts in short bursts of speed. It has a top speed of 32 km/h (20 mph).

NIGHT HUNTERS

As night falls you set up infrared lights and wait silently to see what you can catch on film. Suddenly there's a roar, and sounds of a scuffle. A pack of *Troodon* surround a *Triceratops*! The *Troodon* pounce with their tearing, sickle-shaped claws and serrated teeth – but the *Triceratops* puts up a tough fight. Soon the pack gives up, leaving to find easier game.

The plant-eating *Triceratops* relies on its sharp, 3 ft-(1 m-) long horns to scare off the attackers.

Troodon is seen as the cleverest dinosaur, with the biggest brain in proportion to its body weight.

Troodon is an agile hunter with sharp claws on its hands and its feet.

Meaning of name: Wounding tooth
Height: 3 ft 4 in (1 m)
Length: 6 ft 6 in (2 m)
Family: Troodontidae
Period: Late Cretaceous
Weight: 100 lb (45 kg)
Found in: USA
Diet: Meat

Large, forward-facing eyes mean *Troodon* can judge distances easily. It seems to have good nocturnal vision.

SEEING IN THE DARK

▶ Big eyes suggest good nocturnal vision. The 1.5 ft- (0.5 m-) high *Dromaeosaurus* has huge eyes for the size of its body.

▼ Scientists measure rings of bone in the fossils of dinosaur eyes to estimate how well they could see in the dark. *Velociraptors* were probably among the dinosaurs that hunted at night.

▲ Eye fossil evidence suggests herbivores, such as *Diplodocus*, might have grazed at night too. To keep their vast bodies alive, long grazing hours may have been necessary.

TERRIFYING TYRANT

Your early morning alarm is a blood-curdling roar. You grab your camera, start up the ATV and race towards the sound. It's the biggest dino movie star of them all: *Tyrannosaurus rex*. The monster's strong jaws pick up and shake its victim, an *Iguanodon*. The 'tyrant lizard' uses its fang-like teeth to rip through the skin.

Tyrannosaurus teeth can crush bone. They can be up to 9 in (23 cm) long.

Stretch your arms wide and the length from fingertip to fingertip is about the length of a *Tyrannosaurus* jaw — 4 ft 6 in (1.4 m).

Tyrannosaurus rex is the best known of all the dinosaurs.

Meaning of name: Tyrant lizard king
Height: 19 ft 7 in (6 m)
Length: 45 ft (14 m)
Family: Tyrannosaur
Period: Late Cretaceous
Weight: 7.7 tons (7,000 kg)
Found in: North America
Diet: Meat

Tyrannosaurus' arms are too short to reach their mouths. However, they can be used for clutching prey or for steadying themselves as they stand up.

KILLERS' TEETH

▶ *Giganotosaurus'* teeth are smaller and narrower than the *Tyrannosaurus'* bone-crushers. However, they are better for slicing into the flesh of its prey.

▶ *Acrocanthosaurus* has 68 long, knife-like teeth. Like many theropods' teeth, they are curved and serrated. They are constantly shed and replaced by new teeth that grow in rows.

▶ *Dilophosaurus* has the teeth of a scavenger rather than a killer. The weak jaw and sharp teeth are better for plucking meat from a corpse and lack the strength to stab or grab a living dinosaur.

BATTLE TAILS

Another monster lumbers into view – an *Ankylosaurus*. The *T. rex* seems confused by the sudden appearance of this new opponent. As the predator hesitates, the *Ankylosaurus* swings its muscular tail towards its head. You duck as it whizzes past!

A two-legged predator like *T. rex* is especially vulnerable to *Ankylosaurus'* deadly club.

Ankylosaurus' back and sides are covered with thick, protective plates. The *T. rex* aims to toss it onto its back.

WEAPON TAILS: CLUBS, WHIPS AND SPIKES

***Ankylosaurus* is one of the most heavily plated dinosaurs ever found.**

Meaning of name: Stiff lizard
Height: 4 ft (1.2 m)
Length: 23 ft (7 m)
Family: Ankylosauridae
Period: Late Cretaceous
Weight: 4.4 tons (4,000 kg)
Found in: Canada, USA
Diet: Plants

The knob at the end of the *Ankylosaurus'* tail is made up of bony plates fused together.

The 'handle' of the club is made up of tendons which have partly turned to bone (ossified).

▶ **Tail clubs** Members of the ankylosaurid family, such as *Ankylosaurus*, are the best-known users of tail clubs. However, they are also used by dinosaurs such as the long-necked *Shunosaurus*.

◀ **Whip tails** *Brachiosaurus* flick out their long tails in a whip-like motion, knocking down predators. This gives them the opportunity to trample on their enemies while they are off-balance.

▶ **Tail spikes** Some plant-eaters, such as *Stegosaurus*, have tails ending with spikes. When threatened, a *Stegosaurus* will plant its back legs squarely, and use its front legs to swing its whole body, giving extra momentum to its tail.

FEET FIGHTERS

The epic battle ends in stalemate, and the *Tyrannosaurus* and *Ankylosaurus* leave, blood pouring from cuts and bites. As you walk back to the ATV, a group of fast-moving predators bursts through the bushes. These sleek raptors – called *Deinonychus* – are about your height, and they move fast. You only just make it to your ATV in one piece!

To bring down a smaller target, a raptor stabs a sickle claw into its victim, then drags it in a backwards or downwards motion across its flesh.

Deinonychus' sickle claws are so large they have to be raised when the dinosaur runs.

Deinonychus is far from the biggest dinosaur on the planet, but its intelligence, agility and group hunting tactics make it one of the most fearsome.

Meaning of name: Terrible claw
Height: 5 ft (1.5 m)
Length: 10 ft (3 m)
Family: Dromaeosauridae
Period: Late Cretaceous
Weight: 175 lb (80 kg)
Found in: USA
Diet: Meat

CRUEL CLAWS

▼ The second toe on the *Deinonychus'* hind foot is unusually large – over 4.7 in (12 cm) long – and shaped like a sickle.

▼ **Velociraptor** is probably the most famous raptor. However, it is often misrepresented as being as tall as *Deinonychus*; in fact it is only 3 ft (1 m) tall.

When a pack of *Deinonychus* jumps on a large victim, they use their hook claws like crampons. As they climb upwards, they tear at vulnerable spots with their sharp teeth.

◄ **Troodon** is notable not just for its sickle claws, but also for its teeth, which have serrated sides like a saw.

SCAVENGING SWARM

Time to play it safe for a while. You drive the ATV up a sandy slope, and build a shelter from branches. After a while, a swarm of *Coelophysis* rushes down the slope. Their tails sweep side-to-side like rudders. You follow, and see that they have discovered a carcass. Your camera records how they share their prey; some act as lookouts, while others take turns to eat.

These slim hunters with long tails and long necks are built to run fast. Like birds, they have hollow bones to keep them lightweight.

Coelophysis are not only hunters but probably scavengers too. Fossil contents of a *Coelophysis* stomach suggest that they could even be cannibals.

Coelophysis are known to gather together in packs. They may do this during the breeding season, and also to protect each other while feeding.

There is evidence that *Coelophysis* lived in packs. A flash flood in Mexico revealed the fossils of lots of *Coelophysis* that died together.

Meaning of name: Hollow form
Height: 4 ft 4 in (1.3 m)
Length: 10 ft (3 m)
Family: Coelophysoidea
Period: Late Triassic
Weight: 65 lb (30 kg)
Found in: USA
Diet: Meat

STRENGTH IN NUMBERS?

▼ Sauropod tracks show that the vulnerable young travel with older sauropods of the same species for safety.

▼ Gazelle-like in speed and size, *Hypsilophodon* find greater safety in numbers, as they can keep a better look-out for approaching hunters.

▼ Around 3,500 fossil bones (including 14 skulls) of *Pachyrhinosaurus* have been found in one area of Alberta. They migrate in herds seasonally, in search of food.

CRESTED KILLER

A clunk... a huge weight... and suddenly you're knocked to the dusty ground. The roaring *Dilophosaurus* seem to be in a panic, and race past at about 25 mph (40 km/h). Fortunately, they don't notice you. What are they running from?

Dilophosaurus' dew claw is an unusual feature. It is similar to the dew claw found on the back of each leg on pet dogs and cats.

Weak jaws mean a weak bite, so this killer probably relies on its sharp claws to bring down its prey.

Dilophosaurus is the largest predator of the early Jurassic period, about 200 million years ago.

Meaning of name: Two-ridged lizard
Height: 5 ft (1.5 m)
Length: 20 ft (6 m)
Family: Coelophysoidea
Period: Early Jurassic
Weight: 100 lb (450 kg)
Found in: USA
Diet: Meat

The double crest on the head of *Dilophosaurus* was probably for show, perhaps to make it look taller and more aggressive, and to attract a mate.

HOW MUCH DO WE KNOW?

What do we really know about the appearance of creatures like *Dilophosaurus*?

▶ The crests have never been found attached to the skull, but their position on top of the head is accepted by most scientists as likely to be correct.

▶ Some models of *Dilophosaurus* are covered with hair. Some evidence of hair-like and feather coverings have been found for some prehistoric creatures, such as the bird-like *Archaeopteryx*.

▼ *Dilophosaurus* have been shown with a retractable neck frill, for example in the movie *Jurassic Park*. There is no evidence of them having had frills, although some reptiles alive today do.

AMBUSH!

You run up over the bank to see the creature the *Dilophosaurus* were terrified of. An *Albertosaurus* – a smaller relative of *Tyrannosaurus rex* – is lumbering along a lakeside. Just as you raise the camera, there's a roar and a splash. A *Deinosuchus* lunges up from the water and grabs its neck. The horror of it makes your head spin.

Another name for *Deinosuchus* is *Phobosuchus*, which means 'horror crocodile'. With a deadly gigantic 6.5 ft- (2 m-) long head, and an estimated body length of 33 ft (10 m), it's no wonder!

Albertosaurus was probably able to run at 25 mph (40 km/h) in spite of its size. Like *T. rex*, its teeth were not adapted to chewing, so it swallowed meat in large chunks.

Albertosaurus is a powerful killer and was one of the most common predators in Cretaceous North America.

Meaning of name: Alberta lizard
Height: 11 ft (3.4 m)
Length: 30 ft (9 m)
Family: Tyrannosauridae
Period: Late Cretaceous
Weight: 2.8 tons (2,500 kg)
Found in: North America
Diet: Meat

The *Deinosuchus* is a terrifying crocodile that hides in muddy waters, ambushing dinosaurs and snapping up turtles.

KILLING THE KILLERS

In Cretaceous times, hungry creatures lurked in wetland areas, waiting for passing dinosaurs.

▶ The 100 curved, bone-crunching teeth of the *Deinosuchus* can grasp the throat of a meat-eating dinosaur as it lowers its head to drink.

◀ Cretaceous crocodiles have eyes that can look up out of the water for prey, while their bodies are hidden under the water.

▼ The largest ever crocodile, *Sarcosuchus*, lives in Cretaceous times. Its conical teeth are perfectly shaped for grabbing small dinosaurs and holding them underwater until they drown, ready to be eaten.

ENDGAME

As you set off back to your ATV, the sky suddenly fills with fire. What's happening? A stampede of terrified dinosaurs thunders towards you... and everything goes black. When you come to, you find yourself on a boat heading home, clutching your camera. Perhaps you passed out and the fire-filled sky was all a dream. Or perhaps you just witnessed a new extinction of the dinosaurs.

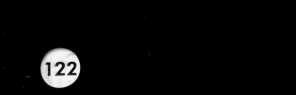

WHAT KILLED THE DINOSAURS?

After ruling the Earth for 150 million years, the dinosaurs all suddenly died 65 million years ago. There are many theories as to what happened.

◀ A vast asteroid or comet may have collided with the Earth, causing a massive explosion, dust clouds and shock waves. All around the world, plants and animals would have died.

▶ Scientists have discovered a vast crater in Mexico that probably formed when an asteroid or comet hit the Earth 65 million years ago. Its 112-mile (180-km) width suggests a catastrophic impact.

▼ In India there were huge volcanic eruptions at the time the dinosaurs died. Vast clouds of ash and dust may have screened out the sun. Plants would have died, then the plant-eaters, and finally the meat-eaters.

KILLER SAFARI REPORT

When you get home, you tell everyone about your safari experience. Crowds gather to hear of your terrifying encounters with killer dinosaurs. When you screen your film, gasps of disbelief fill the auditoriums. The images that get the biggest screams are those of the infamous *Tyrannosaurus rex*!

As you discovered, killers come in all sizes. The small swarming dinosaurs were as deadly as the huge, stumbling monsters. A swipe from the sickle-shaped claw of a 3.3 ft (1 m) *Troodon* could kill you as quickly as a bite from a 16 ft (5 m) *Allosaurus*.

- *Tyrannosaurus rex* - 19 ft 7 in (6 m)
- *Allosaurus* - 16 ft 5 in (5 m)
- *Albertosaurus* - 11 ft (3.4 m)
- *Carnotaurus* - 9 ft 10 in (3 m)
- *Human* - 6 ft (1.8 m)
- *Deinonychus* - 5 ft (1.5 m)
- *Dilophosaurus* - 5 ft (1.5 m)
- *Troodon* - 3 ft 3 in (1 m)
- *Compsognathus* - 2 ft 4 in (0.7 m)

While on your safari, you saw creatures from many different parts of the prehistoric past. This chart shows the different periods in which they lived. MYA stands for million years ago.

Compsognathus

Carnotaurus

Troodon

Tyrannosaurus rex

Ankylosaurus

Deinonychus

Albertosaurus

Dilophosaurus

Allosaurus

Coelophysis

TODAY	
QUATERNARY	1.5 mya
TERTIARY	65 mya
CRETACEOUS	150 mya
JURASSIC	205 mya
TRIASSIC	250 mya
PERMIAN	290 mya
CARBONIFEROUS	355 mya
DEVONIAN	410 mya
SILURIAN	440 mya
ORDOVICIAN	510 mya
CAMBRIAN	570 mya
PRECAMBRIAN	4,600 mya

GLOSSARY

abdomen The core part of an animal's body, from which the head and limbs extend.

air current A body of moving air, such as a breeze or a wind.

air sacs Pockets inside the lungs that are used for storing air. Some animals, such as birds, have air sacs in other parts of their bodies.

asteroid A rocky object that orbits the Sun. Asteroids can crash into other planets, such as Earth.

belemnites Fossil shells that are several inches long, similar to the shell of a cuttlefish.

binocular vision The way in which the world is seen through two forward-facing eyes, which helps an animal judge distance.

camouflage Markings that make something blend into its setting so that it cannot be seen so easily.

cannibals Animals that eat the flesh of their own kind.

Carboniferous A prehistoric period 355 million years ago in which there were many swamps and forests.

carcass The body of a dead creature.

carrion Flesh from a creature that has died, and a source of food for some animals, such as hyenas.

clam A large shellfish with two main parts to its shell, similar to an oyster.

colonies Groups of animals living together in a certain area.

comet An object of ice and dust that travels in space and forms a tail of gas and dust as it passes close to the Sun.

conical A round, pointed shape such as an ice-cream cone.

conifer trees Trees that have needle-shaped leaves and bear cones; examples today are fir and pine trees.

coprolite A fossilized piece of dung.

coral reef A ridge in warm, shallow seas made up of masses of hardened material from the skeletons of tiny sea creatures.

counterweight A weight that acts as a balance, and stops an object or animal from falling over.

courtship A performance that some animals put on to show possible mates that they are strong and healthy.

crest A body part that sticks out from an animal's head.

Cretaceous A prehistoric period in which mammals and giant dinosaurs such as *Tyrannosaurus rex* lived. This period began 150 million years ago and ended with the mass extinction of the dinosaurs 65 million years ago.

cycad A type of palm tree that was common in the Jurassic age.

Devonian A prehistoric period between 410 and 355 milion years ago. This time was also known as the Age of Fishes, when the oceans were warm and filled with many types of evolving fish.

dew claw A claw that does not reach the ground but is positioned higher than the foot, at the back of the leg.

dorsal fin An upright flipper rising up from the back of a fish, which is used for steering and stability.

ellipsoid Oval in shape.

evergreens Plants that have green leaves all year round.

evolve To develop gradually or naturally.

exoskeleton The hard covering some animals have to protect and support their body. Animals with an exoskeleton, such as insects and scorpions, do not have an internal skeleton.

extinct Not existing anymore; for example, dinosaurs and pterosaurs are extinct.

fibrous Made up of stringy material.

filtering Extracting food, such as tiny fish, from water by passing it through sieve-like parts of the mouth.

food chain A group of living things that are linked by what eats what; an example of a food chain is a fox eating a rat, and the rat eating an insect, and the insect eating a plant.

fossils Prehistoric remains such as bones or traces such as footprints that have become preserved in rock.

frill A bony area that is found around the neck of a dinosaur.

gills The parts in a fish's body that are used for breathing.

hibernating Going to sleep for a long time just as an animal like a badger or bear goes to sleep during the winter.

hoaxes Tricks played on people.

insulation A way of keeping warm; for example, feathers insulate birds by keeping the warm in and the cold out.

Jurassic A prehistoric period between 205 and 150 million years ago, during which a huge number of dinosaurs lived.

living fossil A plant or creature that lives today but also lived in prehistoric times in a similar form.

mammals Animals that give birth to live young and feed their young milk. They are warm-blooded.

membrane A part of a creature's body that is similar to a thin skin.

mummified Preserved in a way that slows down the process of decay. The Egyptians famously mummified their pharaohs, but mummification also happens in nature.

nocturnal vision The ability to see well in the dark.

GLOSSARY CONTINUED

omnivorous Able to eat both plants and meat.

palaeontologist A person who studies prehistoric times and evidence such as fossils and rocks.

plates Bony sections on the outer body of a dinosaur that form a protective covering, or stand up from the spine as on a *Stegosaurus*.

parasites Plants or animals that live on or in another, from which they get their food.

predator An animal that hunts other animals to kill and eat.

prey An animal that is hunted by other animals for food.

scales Overlapping plates that form a protective outer layer on creatures such as fish and snakes.

scavenger A creature that feeds on animals that are already dead.

school A large number of fish swimming together in a group.

serrated With a jagged edge, like the edge of a saw.

shock waves A violent change in air pressure that travels outwards from an explosion, causing damage and destruction.

sickle A curved shape like the sickle tool, which was used on farms for cutting crops.

skin impressions The shapes made by the surface of the skin, for example the shapes of scales or feathers on a dinosaur, which are preserved as fossils.

spoonbill A tall wading bird that has a long bill with a flat tip.

stability Steadiness.

tendons Tough, rope-like tissue in bodies, such as the tissue that attaches muscles to bones.

theropods Two-footed, mainly meat-eating dinosaurs such as *Tyrannosaurus rex* and *Giganotosaurus*.

Triassic A prehistoric period between 250 and 205 million years ago, when many creatures became extinct and others, such as pterosaurs, gradually took their place.

vertebrates Creatures with backbones, such as birds, mammals and reptiles.

warm-blooded Able to maintain body heat without needing to bask in the sun to get warm.

wingspan The measurement from one wingtip to the other, when the wings are outstretched.